To ------

From ------

Other mini giftbooks in this series:
Notebook for a very special Friend
Notebook for a very special Grandmother
Notebook for a very special Husband
Notebook for a very special Mother
Notebook for a very special Sister

Published simultaneously in 1996 by Exley Giftbooks in
the USA and Exley Publications Ltd in Great Britain.

12 11 10 9 8 7 6 5 4 3 2 1

Edited by Helen Exley.
Written by Pam Brown.
Illustrated by Juliette Clarke.
Typeset by Delta, Watford.
Printed in Singapore.

Exley Publications Ltd, 16 Chalk Hill, Watford, Herts WD1 4BN, UK.
Exley Giftbooks, 232 Madison Avenue, Suite 1206, NY 10016, USA.

NOTEBOOK

For a very special
DAUGHTER

Written by Pam Brown
Illustrated by Juliette Clarke

EXLEY
NEW YORK · WATFORD, UK

Thanks for all the cards – hand drawn or by Renoir.
For all the parcels – knobbly or beribboned.
For all the hurried kisses – smelling of chocolate or Chanel.
For remembering.

. . . I'm most proud of your being just *you*.
'Success' would be an extra – but you are
special to me *whatever* you do.

_____

_____

_____

_____

_____

_____

_____

_____

_____

_____

_____

. . . like it or not, we are bound to one another.
It is the lightest of links – so light that sometimes
we seem to forget it altogether.
But it is stronger than life itself.

One tiny tug will have me dropping any
masterpiece on which I am engaged – you are,
above everything, the heartbeat of my life.

When I am feeling weary
and all the world is dreary
with thin incessant rain,
I think about my daughter,
her brightness and her laughter,
and life comes right again.

Never forget – you're not just special to me.
You're special. And that's that.

_____

_____

_____

_____

_____

_____

_____

_____

_____

_____

_____

_____

_____

_____

_____

_____

_____

_____

_____

_____

_____

_____

_____

_____

_____

Thank you for having given me the chance to make
mud pies again, to paddle in the sea, to sail toy
boats, to ride the fairground horses . . . .

Thank you for bringing back fun to all our lives.

Thank you for believing my birthday cakes were magical, my paintings amazing and my stories were the best in the world

Sometimes when I'm feeling particularly useless
you give me sound advice – which I once gave you.
It cheers me up no end.

The best thing you have given me is your friendship.

A child gives us our own first times all over again.

Thank you for reawakening wonder.

Thank you for wilting dandelions,
for·twigs of lambstails, for wet pebbles,
for fluff-covered toffees, for sticky kisses.

Thank you for showing me, when I thought
my mothering days were over, that the best
days between us are only just beginning.

There is nothing, absolutely nothing that can cheer up
a dismal evening of TV repeats and yesterday's leftovers
more successfully than a phone call from a daughter.

You have to fight your own battles, love. But I'm here in your corner with the bucket and sponge.

_____

_____

_____

_____

_____

_____

_____

_____

_____

_____

_____

. . . there are things I cannot stick together,
or heal with a hug . . . I wish I had some magic
that could make such things come right. .
All I can do is be here. Always.

My hope for you is that all your life you will
go on being astonished and delighted
by the world about you.

_____

_____

_____

_____

_____

_____

_____

_____

_____

_____

_____

I wish you your own places, your own
adventures, your own loves.

No, love, I don't dream of wealth and success
for you. Only a job you like, skills you can
perfect, enthusiasms to lighten your heart,
friends and love in abundance.

Dear, I hope that when you are very, *very* old
you can look back and say "Heavens. That was
a *lovely* life."

I wish you happy and secure and comfortable and wise.
But not yet. Get the adventures in first.

_____

_____

_____

_____

_____

_____

_____

_____

_____

_____

_____

How can I wish you anything? Save that you find what
you want to do and do it. Well.

_____

_____

_____

_____

_____

_____

_____

_____

_____

_____

_____

_____

_____

What do I *most* wish for you?
A belief in the fundamental worth of human kind, and that,
my dear, includes yourself.

I wish you a daughter just like you.